MACHINES AT WORK

On the Water

IAN GRAHAM

QED Publishing

Copyright © QED Publishing 2006

First published in the UK in 2006 by
QED Publishing
A Quarto Group company
226 City Road
London EC1V 2TT
www.qed-publishing.co.uk

A Catalogue record for this book is available from the British Library.

ISBN 978 1 84538 470 8

Written by Ian Graham
Designed by Calcium
Editor Sarah Eason
Foldout illustration by Ian Naylor
Picture Researcher Joanne Forrest Smith

Publisher Steve Evans
Editorial Director Jean Coppendale
Art Director Zeta Davies

Printed and bound in China

Picture credits
Key: t = top, b = bottom, c = centre, l = left, r = right, FC = front cover

Action Images/Just Add Water 14-15; **Aircraft Carriers and Escort Carriers Archive** (www.navsource.org)/28, FC; **Alamy**/Buzz Pictures 23BR, /Picpics 22-23; **Corbis**/Bohemian Nomad Picture Makers/Kevin R Morris 3, 25T, /Jacques M Chenet 21CR, /Kevin Fleming 11BR, /Stephen Frink 32BL, /Philippe Giraud/Sygma 4BC, /Rowan Griffiths/Stringer/Reuters 6-7, /Stephen Hird/Reuters 13BR, /Daniel Joubert 7TL, /Martin Jones; **Ecoscene** 22BL, /Colin McPherson 10BC, /James Marshall 8-9, /Grafton Marshall Smith 15TC, /Stephanie Maze 24BR; **The Military Picture Library**/Robin Adshead 30-31, /Tim Pannell 15C, /Reuters 4-5, /Neil Rabinowitz 13TL, 15BR, /Steve Raymer 16, 21, /Joel W Rogers 11TL, 21TL, /Nigel Rolstone; **Cordaiy Photo Library** 9TR, /Michael St Maur Shell 24-25, /H Schmied/Zefa 23TL, /Tom Wager/SABA 5TL, /Ralph White 32-33, /Yogi Inc/Robert Y Kaufman 29CL; Crown Copyright/MOD/Dave Griffiths 27BR, /Ritchie Harvey 31TL, /Darren Macdonald 27TR Images from www.photos.mod.uk Reproduced with the permission of the Controller of Her Majesty's Stationary Office; **Deep Flight** 33BC; **Getty Images**/AFP/Rod Taylor 10-11, /Clive Mason 12-13;/Irish Ferries 8BL; P&O Ferries 7BR; **US Navy**/Dylan Butler 26-27, /John E Gray 31CR, /Inez Lawson 29TR, /Kristopher Wilson 29BR.

Words in **bold** can be found in the Glossary on page 34.

CONTENTS

MACHINES IN WATER

People have travelled on water by boat and ship for thousands of years. Today, **ferries** and **liners** carry passengers all over the world, cargo ships move goods and materials across the oceans, warships fight at sea, **powerboats** compete in exciting races and many people spend their leisure time on small yachts and **cruise ships**. These water machines range from small boats the size of a car, to huge ships the size of a skyscraper lying on its side!

THE PARTS OF A SHIP

The hull is the part of a ship that sits in the water. Narrow-shaped hulls can slice quickly through water, but wider hulls hold more passengers and cargo. The sharp front end of the hull is called the bow and the back end is the stern. The ship's control centre is called the bridge. This is raised high above the rest of the ship to give a good view all around.

All ships, like this cruise ➤ liner, have a bow, a stern, a hull and a bridge.

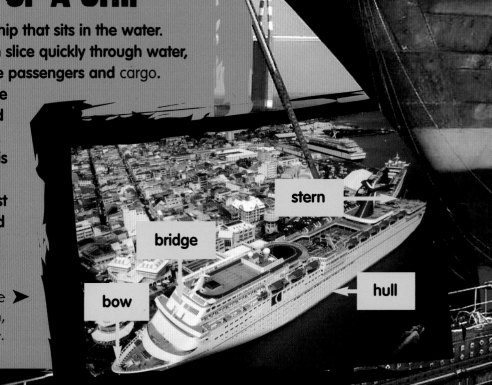

bridge

stern

bow

hull

Water power

Most boats and ships have **propellers** to push them through the water. The propeller of a small boat is so tiny that it can be held in the palm of your hand. The propeller of a big liner or cargo ship can be as large as a house!

▲ Powerful engines drive the huge propellers of a large ship.

◄ Big ships are made by covering a metal frame with sheets of metal.

DE L'ATLANTIQU

OCEAN LINERS

In the days before air travel became popular, travellers crossed the oceans in ships called liners. The great liners had names such as *France*, *Normandie*, *United States* and *Queen Elizabeth*. They competed with each other to cross the Atlantic Ocean in the shortest time. The fastest ones could make the crossing in four or five days.

FACT!

The *RMS Titanic* was built in 1912. It was the biggest and fastest transatlantic liner of its time. Tragically, on its first voyage it hit an iceberg and sank.

The *Queen Mary 2* ➤ set sail for the first time in 2004. With over 1000 cabins, this is the biggest passenger liner built so far.

SUPER LINER

At 345m long – the length of more than 40 double-decker buses – the *Queen Mary 2* can carry over 2500 passengers. The liner is powered by four giant diesel engines and two gas engines similar to aircraft jet engines. Between them, they make enough electricity to light a city!

◄ If you could stand the *Queen Mary 2* on one end, it would be almost as tall as the Empire State Building in New York.

Floating resorts

Modern liners are like floating holiday resorts. They have shops, swimming pools, restaurants and even theatres and cinemas to keep passengers entertained during their voyage.

◄ Modern passenger liners are incredibly luxurious – they are like grand hotels on water!

REDBRIDGE

REDBRIDGE

FERRIES

Ferries are passenger ships that carry people to and from ports on short sea routes. Some ferries carry vehicles as well as passengers. These ships have large doors in either the bow or stern. When the ship docks, the doors open wide and the vehicles inside it drive out. This type of ferry is called a **roll-on**, **roll-off ferry**, or ro-ro for short.

Car ferries can carry ➤ many cars and their passengers. They are like huge floating car parks!

▼ The *Ulysses* weighs more than 50 000 tonnes. This giant ferry has 12 **decks** and is so tall that it towers over other ships.

SUPER FERRIES

Some ferries are huge. *Ulysses* belongs to Irish Ferries and can carry more vehicles than any other ferry in the world. Inside, there are nearly 5km of parking space – that's enough room for over 1300 cars. *Ulysses* can also carry 2000 passengers.

High-speed ferries

Most ferries move quite slowly, but some are designed to be extremely fast. Many of the fast ferries have two hulls instead of one and are called **catamarans**.

With their twin ➤ hulls, catamarans travel twice as fast as other ferries.

FACT!

A ferry called *Cat-Link V* made the fastest ever crossing of the Atlantic Ocean in July 1998. Its voyage took just 2 days, 20 hours and 9 minutes.

FISHING BOATS

Fishing boats are powerful **vessels** with a broad, deep hull that can hold many fish. Small boats work close to the coast and bigger vessels fish further away in the deep ocean. Some fishing boats can freeze their catch on board.

FINDING FISH

The ocean is a big place, so how do fishermen know where to find fish? They use special equipment to help locate large shoals, or groups, of fish. Sonar sends sound waves down into the water and helps the fishermen to 'see' underwater.

▲ Fish shoals found by sonar equipment are shown on a screen on board the fishing boat.

Fishing gear

Fishing boats drag their nets behind them. The shape and size of the nets and their depth in the water depend on the type of fish they catch. Some fish are found near the seabed, others swim in shoals nearer the surface. The fish are trapped in nets and the nets are then pulled up onto the ship.

▲ Fishing boats use powerful **hoists** and **winches** to pull the catch onto the deck.

ELEANOR   19496

Fishing boats need ➤ engines with lots of pulling power to tow the heavy nets through the water.

SAILING BOATS

Sailing boats use wind power to move themselves forward. The most advanced yachts compete in international races and set new speed records. Designed by computers, these boats may have one, two or even three hulls. Their hulls and **masts** are made from modern materials such as **carbon fibre** to make them strong but very light.

The yachts taking part in this ➤ race are all the same, so the race will be won by the most skilful crew.

FACT!
The speed record for a sailing boat is 86kph. It was set in 1993 by a yacht called Yellow Pages Endeavour.

Racing catamarans

Many racing yachts are twin-hulled boats called catamarans. Two thin hulls slice through water faster than one big hull. They also give the boat a wider base and make it harder for the wind to blow it over.

▲ Sailors push racing catamarans to their limit when trying to go as fast as possible in competitions.

SPEED RECORDS

Yachtswoman Ellen MacArthur set a series of speed records in 2004 and 2005 in a specially built trimaran. The boat has a long, slender and lightweight hull to help it slice through the water at speed.

Ellen MacArthur's ➤ record-breaking trimaran is a special water machine. It has a float on each side to stop the wind and waves from rolling it over.

13

POWERBOATS

Powerboats come in all shapes and sizes, from small motor cruisers and sporty speedboats to incredibly fast racing machines. Many powerboats have a sharp, V-shaped hull that slices through the water at top speeds. Others have a flat-bottomed hull that skims the water surface, allowing the boat to travel even faster. These surface skimmers are called **hydroplanes**. Personal water vehicles, better known as jet-skis, also dart about the surf at top speeds, just like floating motorbikes!

Offshore powerboat racers ➤ have incredibly powerful engines and can be up to 5 times more powerful than a family car.

JUST ADD WATER

GUERNSEY

FACT!

The highest speed ever reached on water is 511kph. This record was set in 1978 by Ken Warby in his hydroplane **Spirit of Australia**.

CARGO SHIPS

Most cargo ships are specially built to carry one particular type of cargo. There are many types of cargo ship from oil tankers, **containerships** and gas tankers to coal ships called colliers, **bulk carriers**, grain carriers and ore carriers. About 40 000 cargo ships transport goods and materials all over the world.

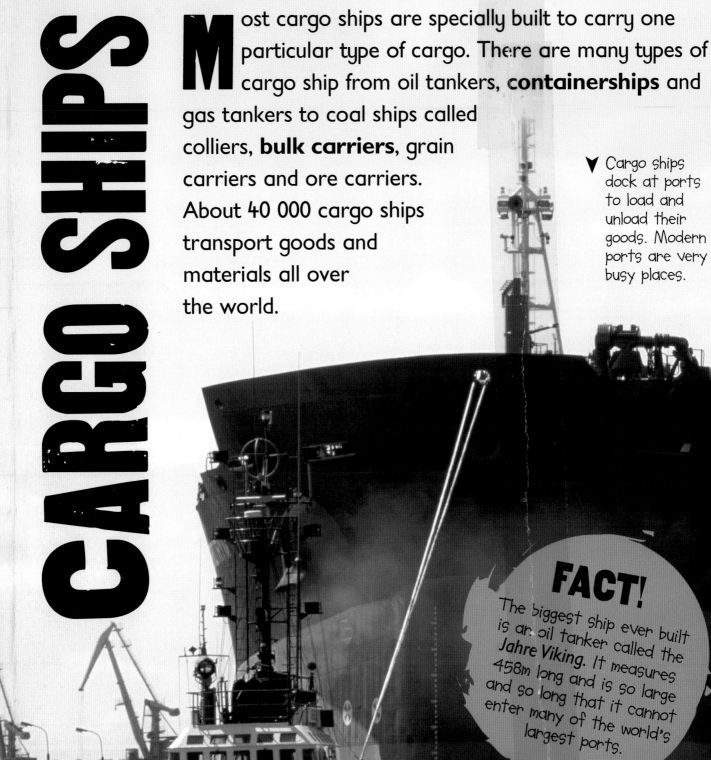

▼ Cargo ships dock at ports to load and unload their goods. Modern ports are very busy places.

FACT!
The biggest ship ever built is an oil tanker called the *Jahre Viking*. It measures 458m long and is so large and so long that it cannot enter many of the world's largest ports.

GAS TANKER

Gas tankers are ships that are designed to carry gas. Before it is loaded onto a tanker, the gas is first cooled to change it into a liquid. Liquid takes up less space, which means the tanker can carry more. Liquid Natural Gas (LNG) and Liquid Petroleum Gas (LPG) are transported like this.

smoke stack releases fumes and smoke from the engines

The tanks of a ➤ gas carrier ship are surrounded by thick **insulation**, which keeps the cargo cold.

NO SMOKING

FIRE STATION

FIRE STATION

Building a cargo ship

The first part of a cargo ship to be built is the keel. The keel is the strongest part of the ship. It runs along the bottom of the hull from the bow to the stern. A frame of steel beams is built upwards from the keel and covered with steel plates to form the hull. Next, the **decks** are added. Finally a crane lifts the bridge and crew cabins into position.

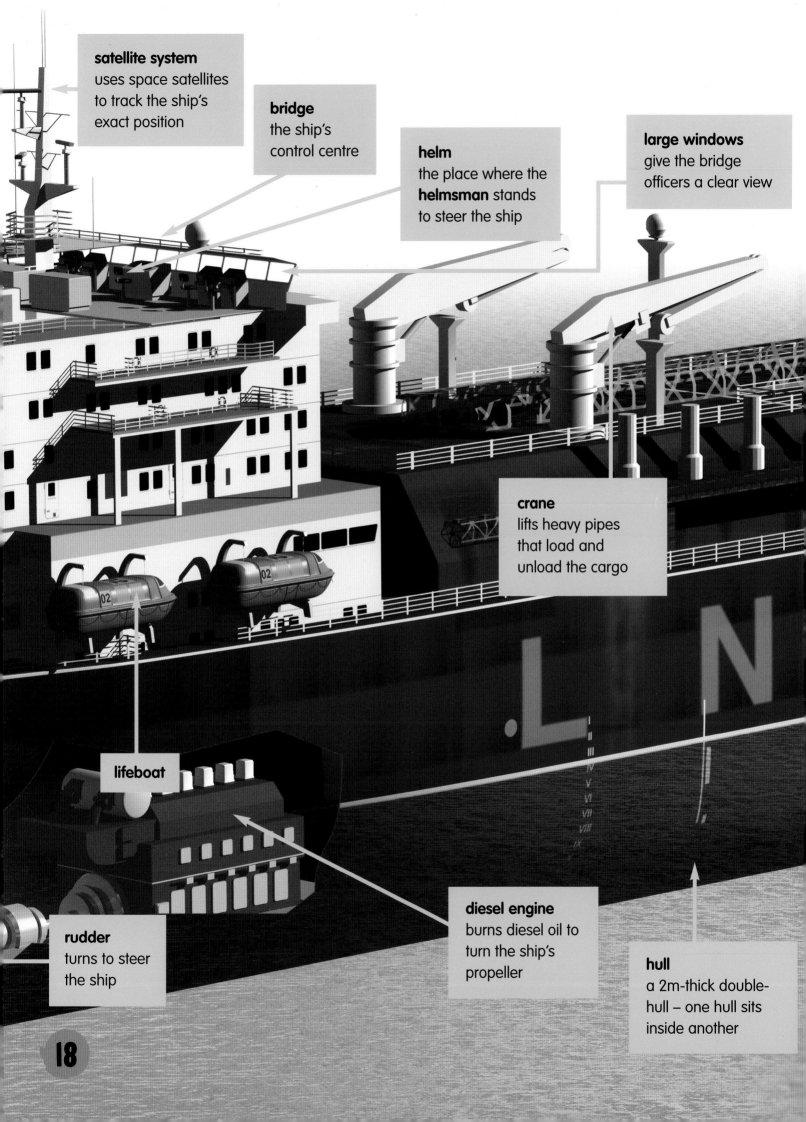

satellite system
uses space satellites to track the ship's exact position

bridge
the ship's control centre

helm
the place where the **helmsman** stands to steer the ship

large windows
give the bridge officers a clear view

crane
lifts heavy pipes that load and unload the cargo

lifeboat

rudder
turns to steer the ship

diesel engine
burns diesel oil to turn the ship's propeller

hull
a 2m-thick double-hull – one hull sits inside another

18

Ski-boats

Some speedboats, called ski-boats, are specially designed for towing water-skiers and **wake-boarder**s through the water at breathtaking speeds. A wide, flat hull allows ski-boats to race at top speed across the surface of the water.

▲ Ski-boats glide over the water surface at top speed. This is called planing.

◄ A jet-ski rider steers by turning the handlebars and leaning to one side.

SKIMMING RACERS

As a hydroplane racing boat picks up speed, it rises up on top of the water – planing like a ski-boat. At top speed, only the propeller and the tips of two floats are in the water.

The fastest racing hydroplanes ► can reach speeds of up to about 320kph.

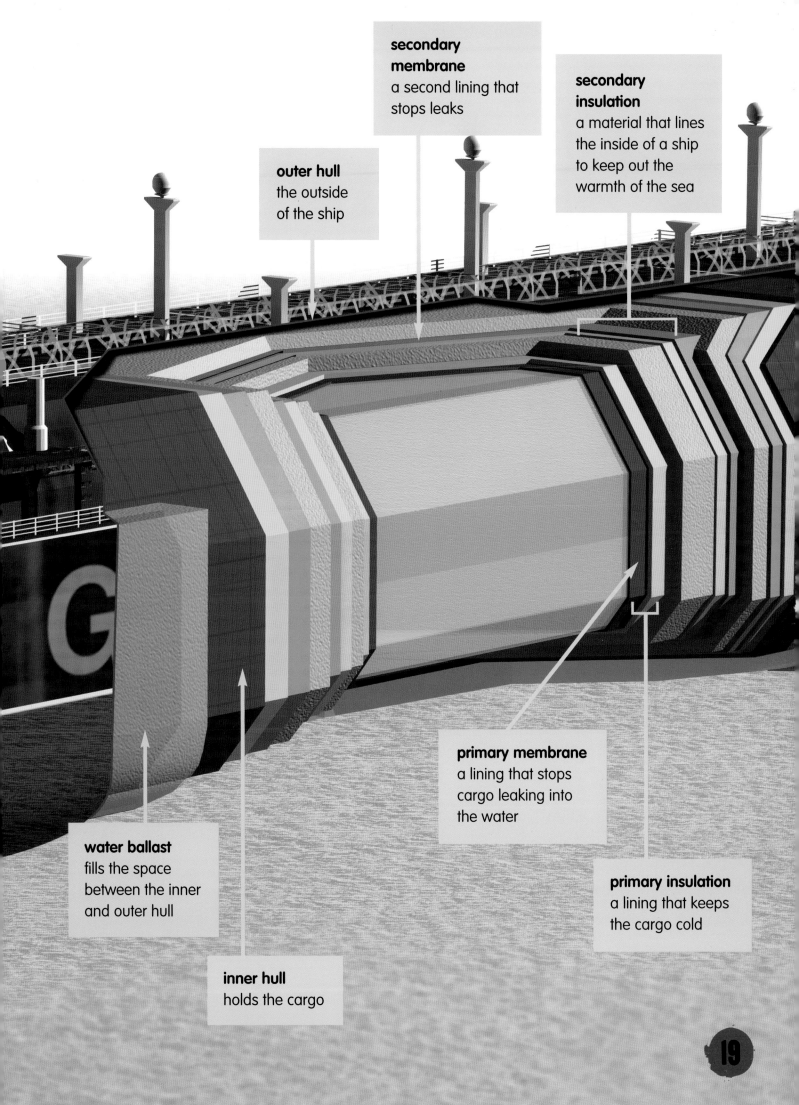

secondary membrane
a second lining that stops leaks

outer hull
the outside of the ship

secondary insulation
a material that lines the inside of a ship to keep out the warmth of the sea

primary membrane
a lining that stops cargo leaking into the water

water ballast
fills the space between the inner and outer hull

primary insulation
a lining that keeps the cargo cold

inner hull
holds the cargo

FLYING BOATS

When a boat moves forwards, water presses against it and slows it down. To travel faster, the hull needs to be out of the water. That's how **hydrofoil**s and **hovercraft** travel. Hydrofoils have underwater wings called **foils**. As they speed up, the hull starts rising and comes out of the water altogether.

With their ➤ underwater wings, hydrofoils provide fast passenger transport on rivers and lakes and between islands.

▼ A Boeing Jetfoil cruises over the water at up to 80kph.

Jetfoils

Jetfoils are hydrofoils powered by **waterjet** engines instead of propellers. They pump water out of the boat's stern at high speed. The boat constantly measures its height above the water and adjusts the angle of the foils to keep it flying along at the same height.

Tugboats

There is little spare space in a busy port. This can make it difficult for big ships to move around. Some cargo ships have extra propellers called **thrusters** to help them turn in a tight space and sometimes dock by themselves. Ships can also be safely moved around by small but powerful boats called **tugboats**.

▲ **Tides** and wind can make a big cargo ship difficult to control. Tugboats often move them in and out of ports.

▼ The job of a port traffic controller is to make sure that ships enter and leave port safely.

TRAFFIC CONTROL

Like many modern ships, cargo ships use satellites to navigate, or find their way around. Radio signals from satellites orbiting the Earth show exactly where ships are located and where they are heading. When cargo ships enter busy shipping lanes near big ports, their movements are strictly controlled to avoid collisions.

bow
designed to be sharp at the
top to cut through waves
and rounded at the bottom
to push through the water

PANAMAX SHIPS

The Panama Canal is a canal that
connects the Pacific Ocean to the Atlantic
Ocean in Panama, Central America. Vessels that
travel through it must be small enough to pass
through the thinnest part of the canal. These
vessels are called Panamax ships. The biggest
ships normally allowed to go through the canal
are 294m long and 32m wide.

▲ Small tugboats help
to guide a long
cargo ship through
a narrow canal.

SUBMERSIBLES

Scientists and underwater explorers sometimes dive in small craft called **submersibles**. A submersible is carried by ship to the place where it is to dive. When it sinks below the waves, small propellers called thrusters move it around underwater. Deep-diving submersibles have just enough room inside for two or three people. They sit inside a compartment shaped like a ball to resist the crushing pressure of the water.

An underwater ➤ scooter rider's head fits inside a clear plastic bubble full of air.

Seeing the sights

Holidaymakers in some parts of the world can visit the seabed in a submersible. They can see the underwater sights, tour a tropical reef or watch divers feeding fish.

BELOW THE WAVES

Submarines have to make themselves heavier to submerge. They do this by letting seawater flood into empty tanks inside them. The biggest submarines have to take in thousands of tonnes of water to submerge. How do they float up to the surface again? By blowing out the water!

▲ A submarine's smooth black hull glides through the water.

Sound safety

Submarines do not have windows, so the crew uses a system called 'sonar' to find their way ahead. By using sonar, the crew can probe the water ahead for silent objects, such as underwater mountains. They can also hear the sounds of nearby ships and submarines, and even whales singing!

▲ A submarine crew uses state-of-the-art technology to work out their depth, speed and direction.

▼ The wings on this Australian Collins class submarine are hydroplanes. They tilt to make the submarine go up or down underwater.

FACT!

The biggest submarines are Russian Typhoon class vessels. They are 171m long and weigh more than 18 500 tonnes!

SUBMARINES

Submarines are the only naval vessels that deliberately sink themselves! They patrol the oceans, hidden beneath the waves. Submarines **submerge** soon after they leave port and stay underwater for up to three months. They only need to come to the surface when the crew runs out of food. Submarines have to be manned 24 hours a day, so there are always at least two crews on board. As one crew sleeps, another runs the submarine.

The biggest ➤ submarines have a crew of more than 150 people.

The island

An aircraft carrier is controlled from a structure on one side of the deck called the island. This keeps the deck clear for planes to land.

The island gives the ship's commander a good ➤ view of the deck and all around the ship.

MEGA CATAPULT

An aircraft carrier's deck is not the same as an airport runway. The deck has a powerful catapult built into it. Each plane is hooked onto the catapult and then hurled along the deck and into the air! Without a catapult, planes would not be moving fast enough to fly by the time they reached the end of the deck.

▲ A carrier's catapult can launch a plane to an amazing speed of 265kph in just two seconds!

Landing by wire

Planes land so fast on the ship that they cannot stop before they run out of deck. Special wires, called **arrester cables**, stretch across the deck. As the plane lands, a hook under its tail catches the cables and stops it travelling forwards.

▲ An aircraft carrier's arrester cables can stop a plane landing at 240kph in less than 100m.

29

AIRCRAFT CARRIERS

The biggest warships ever built are the US Navy's Nimitz class aircraft carriers. These **nuclear-powered warships** weigh an amazing 100 000 tonnes and carry a crew of about 6000. They can hold around 85 aircraft, many of which are kept in a vast **hangar** below deck. When planes are needed they are moved up to the flight deck by four huge lifts.

▼ A Nimitz class aircraft carrier can sail for up to 15 years before its nuclear engines have to be refuelled.

FACT!

The cooks on board a Nimitz class aircraft carrier have to prepare up to 20 000 meals every day!

▲ Modern warships work on their own or together with other ships in a force called a battle group.

◄ Most modern warships travel at speeds of up to 65kph.

SUPPLY SHIPS

Warships do not always have time to visit a port to take fuel, food and other supplies on board. Instead, supplies are delivered to them at sea by other ships. Supply ships include fuel tankers, stores ships, ammunition ships and support ships.

▲ A warship (right) is refuelled at sea by a fuel tanker ship called an oiler (left).

WARSHIPS

Warships were once large, heavily armoured vessels with lots of big guns. Their guns could fire shells over great distances, making them fearsome fighting machines. Today, **missiles** have replaced big guns and the thick, heavy armour has gone, too. Most modern warships are smaller, lighter ships called **cruisers**, **destroyers** and **frigates**. Some warships carry helicopters to search for enemy submarines.

FACT!

A modern cruiser costs over £500 million to build!

flare stack

Gas flare

Oil and gas platforms have lots of safety features to make sure that gas does not burst out of the pipes or storage tanks. Extra gas is allowed to escape through the **flare stack**. Here, the gas is burned to stop it from harming the environment. A small amount burns at the top of the flare stack all the time.

▲ Any extra gas is harmlessly burned off into the sky.

◄ A drilling rig stands high above the water to let waves pass underneath.

FACT!

The Petronius platform in the Gulf of Mexico is one of the world's biggest offshore platforms. It stands 610m tall — that's nearly as high as two Eiffel Towers!

◄ *Alvin* is a submersible that can dive to a depth of 4.5km. It was used to explore the wreck of *RMS Titanic* on the seabed.

FLYING UNDERWATER

A little like balloons, most submersibles sink and surface by making themselves heavier or lighter. A new type of submersible actually 'flies' underwater in the same way that a plane flies through the air – it even has wings!

◄ *Deep Flight 1* is a new kind of submersible with wings. It was developed to explore the deepest parts of the oceans.

33

GLOSSARY

arrester cable a length of wire stretched across the deck of an aircraft carrier to catch the tail hooks of aircraft as they land

bathyscaphe a type of craft that can be submerged and used for deep-sea exploration

bow the front end of a boat or ship

bridge the part of a ship raised high above the deck. The captain commands the ship from the bridge

bulk carrier a type of cargo ship that carries dry materials such as grain, cement or sugar

carbon fibre a strong material made from threads of carbon that have been heated and stretched

cargo goods carried on board a ship or boat

catamaran a boat with two hulls

catapult a machine that can hurl an object into the air. Catapults are used on warships to launch aeroplanes into the air

containership a ship designed to carry containers full of goods

cruise ship a large ship that carries its passengers to many different destinations

cruiser a high-speed warship

decks the floors of a vessel

destroyer a small, heavily armed warship that travels at high speed

ferry a ship that makes short journeys between sea ports

flare stack a tower on an oil rig through which extra gas is released into the air and burned

foils wings on a boat or ship that lift it out of the water so that it can travel at speed

frigate a warship that is often used to protect other warships

gas tanker a ship that carries gas

hangar a place in which aircraft are stored

hoist a machine that can lift something into the air

hovercraft a vessel that travels across water or land on top of a cushion of air

hull the part of a boat or ship that sits in the water

hydrofoil a type of boat or ship that travels above the surface of the water

hydroplane a high-speed racing boat that skims across the surface of the water

liner a large passenger ship that transports people on long-distance sea journeys

mast a tall pole on a ship or a boat that holds up sails or rigging

missile a weapon that is launched at a target

nuclear-powered warship a warship that is driven by nuclear energy

orbit to circle something

powerboat a high-speed boat driven by a powerful engine

propeller part of a ship or boat that moves it through the water. A spinning propeller spins and pushes against the water, thrusting the vessel in the opposite direction.

roll-on, roll-off a ship designed so that cars can drive straight onto or off it

satellite   a machine that travels in space around the world and sends signals back to Earth

sonar   a way of using sound waves to find objects underwater. If an object is found, the sound waves 'bounce' off it to show where it is

stern   the back end of a boat or ship

submarine   a large craft that can dive underwater for days, weeks or even months and come back to the surface again

submerge   dive below the surface of the water

submersible   a small craft that can dive into deep water for short periods

tide   the rise and fall of the sea level

trimaran   a lightweight sailing boat that has three hulls

tugboat   a small but very powerful boat that tows or pushes bigger ships

vessel   a machine that travels on water

wake-boarder   someone who skis behind a ski-boat on a single board

waterjet   a type of engine that works by shooting water out of the back of a ship to push it forwards

winch   a machine used to lift or pull heavy objects

FIND OUT MORE

Websites

Find out the answers to lots of questions about boats:
http://www.boatsafe.com/kids/index.htm

Learn more about boats:
http://www.boatingsidekicks.com/kidsknow/intrknow.htm

See inside a submarine and find out what it's like to dive below the waves:
www.pbs.org/wgbh/nova/subsecrets

Read about lots of different deep-sea machines:
www.pbs.org./wgbh/nova/abyss/frontier/deepsea.html

Find out about Australian and New Zealand boats used in the Pacific Ocean:
http://www.safeboating.org.au/Boating/Kids_in_Boats/Boats_now _and_then.asp

INDEX